This book belongs to:

Jonah

Age:

www.ingramcontent.com/pod-product-compliance
Lightning Source LLC
Chambersburg PA
CBHW081553280526
45788CB00011B/3462
9781099346415